# BOOK ANALYSIS

Written by Evelyne Marotte
Translated by Rebecca Neal

# The Belly of Paris

## BY ÉMILE ZOLA

Bright
≡Summaries.com

# ÉMILE ZOLA

FRENCH WRITER AND JOURNALIST

- **Born in Paris in 1840.**
- **Died in Paris in 1902.**
- **Notable works:**
  - *Nana* (1880), novel
  - *The Ladies' Paradise* (1883), novel
  - *Germinal* (1885), novel

Émile Zola was born in 1840 and died in 1902. He is considered to be one of the greatest French novelists of the 19th century. He was also the leading figure of naturalism, a movement which sought to apply the experimental scientific methods of the time to literature: after observing reality, Zola would put forward a hypothesis and test it through experimentation in his books. This aesthetic can be seen in particular in *Les Rougon-Macquart*, a cycle of 20 novels which constitutes his most important work and met with major success, in spite of many criticisms.

Zola was also famous for his social and political

stances, which often provoked strong reactions. The best-known of these concerns the Dreyfus affair; his pamphlet *J'accuse* ("I accuse") was a major contributing factor to the pardoning of the Jewish officer Alfred Dreyfus (1859-1935).

# THE BELLY OF PARIS

## THE STORY OF LES HALLES IN PARIS

- **Genre:** novel
- **Reference edtion:** Zola, É. (2009) *The Belly of Paris*. Trans. Nelson, B. Oxford: Oxford University Press.
- **1st edition:** 1873
- **Themes:** food, revolution, French society, politics, conspiracy

*The Belly of Paris* was first published in 1873 and is the third novel in Zola's *Les Rougon-Macquart* cycle. Each of Zola's novels explores one aspect of 19th-century society; in this case, he describes the architecture and workings of Les Halles, the new market in central Paris, in painstaking detail.

*The Belly of Paris* is one of Zola's early works, and the theory of the experimental novel is particularly visible in the skilful descriptions which serve as a vibrant tribute to the impressionist painters.

# SUMMARY

## CHAPTER 1

Madame François, a market gardener from Nanterre, is travelling to Les Halles in Paris when she sees Florent in a ditch, unconscious and half dead from hunger. She takes him to the capital in her cart, which is filled with fresh vegetables.

Florent had previously been sent to the penal colony of Cayenne after being wrongfully convicted of killing a woman during the political upheaval of December 1851. However, he managed to escape, and has spent the past two years trying to secretly return to Paris.

> **GOOD TO KNOW: NAPOLEON III's COUP D'ÉTAT**
>
> As Napoleon III's (1808-1873) term as president of the Second Republic of France was coming to an end, he decided to launch a coup d'état on 2 December 1851 to remain in power in France and restore the Empire.

Public opinion supported him in this, as Parliament was in disarray. On the day of the coup, the leaders of the opposition were arrested and imprisoned. Some fighting broke out, particularly in the countryside, but it did not last for long. The Second Empire was proclaimed on 14 January 1852.

The cart reaches Les Halles, the ten brand-new steel and glass pavilions that make up the "belly of Paris". The painter Claude Lantier soon meets Florent and leads him to the Rue Pirouette. Claude seems to know the street well. We are introduced to some of the people of Les Halles, including the Méhudins, who are fishwives; Monsieur Lebigre, who runs the local bar; and Marjolin and Cadine, two orphans who grew up in Les Halles and are the soul of the market.

## CHAPTER 2

Through a flashback, we learn Florent's story. After the death of his father, he began studying law, until his mother, the family's sole breadwinner, died. He then abandoned his studies to look after his little brother Quenu, and the two moved to Paris together. In Paris, Quenu developed an interest in rotisserie because of the poultry seller Gavard, while Florent became involved in politics and took part in the republican uprisings of 1848 and 1851. He got caught up in an exchange of gunfire and was wrongfully accused of killing a young woman who fell dead at his feet. He was then imprisoned at Bicêtre before being deported to a penal colony, while Quenu learnt how to run a charcuterie from his uncle Gradelle.

**GOOD TO KNOW: THE FRENCH REVOLUTION OF 1848**

The French Revolution of 1848 resulted from the economic crisis that had been ravaging France for two years and the failure of King Louis Philippe I (1773-1850) to intervene and manage the situation. The people rose up and demanded major reform. Following the violence which broke out across the country, the king abdicated and the Second Republic was proclaimed.

Some time later, Gradelle's wife passed away and he took on a girl, Lisa Macquart, to replace her at the shop. When Gradelle died, Quenu and Lisa decided to get married and open their own charcuterie opposite Les Halles, thanks to the money left by Quenu's uncle. Lisa then became known as "the beautiful Lisa" and gave birth to a daughter, Pauline. She stands out as a beacon of success and honour in the neighbourhood.

After escaping from Cayenne, Florent reaches France, then Paris. In 1858, he is reunited with his brother in his charcuterie. Lisa offers him his share of the money left by Gradelle, but he refuses it. Florent moves in with Quenu and Lisa.

Florent starts spending time with Gavard, who is also a republican. Gavard is a poultry seller at Les Halles and finds Florent a job as an inspector in the fish market.

## CHAPTER 3

Florent reluctantly accepts the job. He replaces a man called Monsieur Verlaque, to whom he has to give a third of his salary. The fishwives hate him and he struggles to win their acceptance.

Florent meets Gavard and their fellow republicans at Lebigre's bar. He is introduced to Robine, Manoury, Logre and Charvet, their leader, who leads the discussion along with his girlfriend Clémence.

At Les Halles, Florent is forced to intervene during an incident between the Méhudins and the maid who works for Madame Taboureau, the baker. Louise Méhudin, known as "La Belle Normande", decides to exact revenge on him. Florent is teaching her son Muche to read, and Louise decides to invite him to her house for lessons, to the great displeasure of her sister Claire, who is secretly in love with him. This tactic allows her to make peace with Florent and start seeing him regularly, in order to make Lisa jealous. In this way, she hopes to cause a rift between Florent and his sister-in-law.

When Mademoiselle Saget, the local gossip, tells Lisa that Quenu has been following his brother to Lebigre's bar to plot, Lisa gets angry with her husband and starts trying to force Florent out of her home.

# CHAPTER 4

Lisa wants to find out more about Florent's political activities. She decides to speak to Gavard and follows Marjolin, who works for him, into the poultry cellars. However, when Marjolin tries to assault her, she strikes him and flees, leaving him unconscious.

Florent and Claude Lantier pay a visit to Madame François, the vegetable seller, in Nanterre and enjoy a pleasant day in the countryside. Claude takes the opportunity to explain his theory of "The Battle of the Fat and the Thin" (p. 190) to Florent.

# CHAPTER 5

Lisa is reluctant to report her brother-in-law to the authorities, so she seeks advice from Father Roustan at the Saint-Eustache church. She also searches Florent's bedroom and finds revolutionary writings. At the same time, her daughter Pauline is playing with Muche, but their game ends badly: Pauline is in tears when Mademoiselle Saget intervenes. Mademoiselle Saget walks Pauline home, but only so that she can get the girl to talk. Pauline reveals that she overheard her parents say that Florent had spent time in a penal colony. This is all the information Mademoiselle Saget needs to spread the rumour, starting with the Lecœurs, who are dairywomen at the market. Before long, all the women at Les Halles have turned against Florent, except Louise Méhudin, who wants to marry him.

Meanwhile, Florent is planning an uprising without knowing that Logre is a pathological liar and Charvet, who is jealous of his charisma, is distancing himself from him.

Lisa goes to the police and reports Florent in order to save her business from the rumour that is endangering it. The police tell her that they already know all about Florent's activities and show her letters of denunciation from Mademoiselle Saget and Mère Méhudin. Lisa is filled with dismay. She returns home and decides not to say anything to her husband.

## CHAPTER 6

The police burst into Lisa and Quenu's house in search of Florent. They ransack his bedroom and lie in wait for him there. Gavard comes to see Florent and is arrested for his complicity in the plot. He has time to give his sister-in-law, the dairywoman Lecœur, the key to the wardrobe where he keeps his savings. She immediately goes to collect the money.

Florent leaves Les Halles and goes back to his room. Like Gavard, he is arrested, but he feels almost relieved because the atmosphere of the market sellers of Les Halles was becoming too much for him to bear.

Shortly afterwards, Lisa and Louise Méhudin make up. The traitor Lebigre marries Louise and opens a tobacco shop, "a long-cherished dream which he had finally been able to realize through the services he had rendered to the authorities" (p. 274). Claude looks on, sickened by the collusion between the market sellers and the police, as Cadine and Marjolin continue their relationship, oblivious to the events unfolding around them.

# CHARACTER STUDY

According to the theory set out by Claude Lantier in Chapter 4, human beings can be divided into two categories, the "Fat" and the "Thin". The only aim of the "Fat" is to get fatter, while the "Thin" are devoured by their will to improve society. They are unable to get fatter and are rejected by the "Fat", who are left uneasy by their thinness. All the characters in *The Belly of Paris* can be placed in one of these two categories.

## THE "FAT" CHARACTERS IN THE CHARCUTERIE

### Quenu

Quenu is Florent's half-brother and does not even have a first name in the novel: he is only referred to by his long-dead father's surname. He was orphaned when his mother died while he was still a child, and raised by Florent. Florent spoiled him, which left him passive and backward and meant that he struggled to choose a vocation. When he visited Gavard's rotisserie and was enraptured by the roast chickens, he finally found his calling: food. His interest was so great that he used the money he inherited from his uncle Gradelle to open his own charcuterie opposite Les Halles. He grew very fat and only worked in the back of the shop, and married Lisa, who now makes all his decisions for him. Throughout the novel, Quenu is shut out of the adult world: nobody tells him about his brother's first arrest and Lisa reports Florent to the police without saying anything to him. He is his wife's puppet, and is naïve and criminally passive. At the end of the novel, when the only person who ever loved and helped him is arrested, all he can do is cry.

## Lisa

She is the eldest daughter of the Macquart family from Plassans. She belongs to the illegitimate branch of the Rougon-Macquart family. She is also the sister of Gervaise, the heroine of *L'Assommoir* (1877). After Gradelle dies, she marries Quenu and gives birth to a daughter, Pauline, who will be the heroine of *The Joy of Living* (1884), the twelfth novel in the *Les Rougon-Macquart* cycle.

Lisa is a "Fat" character and is always impeccably and respectably dressed. She embodies the bourgeois ideal, as she is well fed, serious, impassive and dignified in her appearance. Although she is respected in the neighbourhood, "the beautiful Lisa" is nonetheless consumed by envy: she is jealous of "La Belle Normande", her rival for the admiration of the market sellers of Les Halles. Her behaviour is dictated by her desire to hurt Louise. This can be seen, for example, in her hypocritical attitude towards her brother-in-law Florent, her visit to Father Roustan at Saint-Eustache and her lies to her husband. With Florent's arrest at the end of the novel, she finally triumphs over Louise, which allows her to regain a sense of calm and peace.

She is described as follows by Doctor Pascal, the titular character of the final novel of the *Les Rougon-Macquart* cycle:

> "With Lisa Macquart began the illegitimate branch; appearing fresh and strong in her, as she displayed her portly, prosperous figure, sitting at the door of her pork shop in a light colored apron, watching the central market, where the hunger of a people muttered, the age-long bat-

tle of the Fat and the Lean, the lean Florent, her brother-in-law, execrated, and set upon by the fat fishwomen and the fat shopwomen, even the fat pork-seller herself, honest, but unforgiving, caused to be arrested as a republican who had broken his ban, convinced that she was laboring for the good digestion of all" (*Doctor Pascal*, Chapter 5).

## THE "FAT" CHARACTERS OF THE FISHWIVES' PAVILION: THE MÉHUDINS

Louise and Claire Méhudin and their mother are the three emblematic figures of the fishwives' pavilion.

### Mère Méhudin

Mère Méhudin, a fat, shapeless 65-year-old woman dripping with flashy, tasteless jewellery, is the leader of the fishwives: she makes the rules in Les Halles and at home, where she controls the two daughters who live with her. She hates Florent and mercilessly pursues him from the first time she sets eyes on him because he is thin and because he fines her once he becomes inspector. She emerges triumphant at the end of the novel when Florent is arrested.

## Claire Méhudin

At around 30, Claire is Mère Méhudin's youngest daughter. She is small and blonde, and her physique reveals her fragility and delicateness: Claude Lantier likens her to "some faded saint that had stepped down from a stained glass window into the degraded world of the markets" (p. 107). She struggles to deal with the strong smells of the saltwater fish, so she works at the stall selling freshwater fish. She hates her mother and her older sister. She is secretly in love with Florent and jealous of her sister Louise, but sulks in her room or behind her stall rather than saying anything. By the time she decides to defect from the "Fat" side and join the "Thin" side by warning Florent of his imminent arrest, it is too late. Claire is a victim of her mother's tyranny.

## Louise Méhudin

Louise is the eldest daughter of the family and is nicknamed "La Belle Normande". She is a voluptuous brunette with a "superb bust" (p. 128) who has inherited her mother's domineering personality. She is married to a poor, impotent man who works at the corn market. She has a son, Muche, who is left to his own devices and is "as pretty as an angel and as coarse in his manners as any carter" (p. 116). Florent teaches him to read. Although she is initially hostile towards the young inspector, Louise learns to appreciate this "Thin" character and uses him to exact revenge on Lisa, who has been her rival for as long as anyone can remember.

## THE "FAT" CHARACTERS FROM THE OTHER PAVILIONS: GAVARD AND THE LECŒURS

### Gavard

Gavard is the dominant figure of the poultry market. His name closely resembles the French word *bavard* ("talkative"); as this suggests, he is boastful and very sure of himself. He took in Marjolin, the child who was found in Les Halles, to help him with his work. He is a regular at the meetings in Lebigre's bar, and never misses an opportunity to criticise the current regime. A staunch republican, Gavard is a braggart who seems incapable of discretion: he is never without his pistol and shows it to everyone working at Les Halles.

## Madame Lecœur

According to Lantier, this imposing dairywoman is a frustrated "Fat" character. She is a widow and had her sights set on her brother-in-law Gavard, whose spouse had also died. However, he turned her down and she takes her revenge on him at the end of the novel by opting not to destroy the documents he had asked her to get rid of before the arrival of the police.

## La Sarriette

La Sarriette is the niece of Madame Lecœur, who has taken her in. The young woman works as a fruit seller and is plump, brazen, unscrupulous and unfeeling.

# THE FUTURE "FAT" CHARACTERS OF LES HALLES: CADINE AND MARJOLIN

These two characters embody the soul of Paris's central market. They are both orphans who were found in Les Halles and taken in by market sellers like Mère Chantemesse.

## Marjolin

In a way, Marjolin is the Quasimodo of Les Halles: he is large, well-built, strong and brutal, but at the same time he is simple-minded and naïve. He is at home in Les Halles and spends a lot of time in the poultry cellars, where he takes pleasure in killing pigeons and fowl. He loves Cadine, who he has known his whole life, with an animalistic, fraternal and romantic passion. Although he is violent, he is not dangerous: when he tries to assault Lisa, he is the one who ends up injured and hospitalised.

## Cadine

Cadine is a thin, lively, cunning and feral little girl with matted brown hair. She should really be a

"Thin" character, but she cannot escape the belly of Paris, where she has grown up, and is content to take each day as it comes. She is uneducated and remains a street vendor.

Other secondary characters also form part of the "Fat" category in *The Belly of Paris*. These include the unscrupulous bar owner Lebigre, who betrays Florent and his customers and exploits his waitress, Rose; Auguste and Augustine Landois, who work at the charcuterie before getting married and opening their own shop at the end of the novel; and the baker Madame Taboureau, who sends her maid to do her shopping at Les Halles.

## THE "THIN" CHARACTERS

There are few "Thin" figures in this novel focused on good food, but they are the most important characters.

### Claude Lantier

Claude Lantier is Lisa Quenu's nephew and the cousin of Étienne Lantier, the hero of *Germinal* (1885). In *The Belly of Paris* he represents the figure of the artist, and later on he is the protagonist of *The Masterpiece* (1886), the fourteenth novel in the *Les Rougon-Macquart* cycle. He is thin and bony, and has a beard, a kind face, a delicate nose and pale eyes. He likes Florent and gives him a warm welcome when he arrives in Paris, taking him to the Rue Pirouette and showing him the brand-new neighbourhood of Les Halles, where his keen painter's eye finds many sources of inspiration. Claude wants to paint modernity and provide an unvarnished depiction of reality, which makes him similar to the realist and impressionist French painters such as Courbet (1819-1877), Manet (1832-1883) and Monet (1840-1926), who Zola admired and praised in his critical writings. On the way back from spending the day at Nanterre with Madame François, he outlines his naturalist theory of "The Battle of the Fat and the Thin" to Florent.

## Florent

Florent is a thin man who is always dressed in black. He does not go unnoticed in the "Fat" world of *The Belly of Paris*. He is too generous and selfless to accept his share of Gradelle's money, which Lisa offers him when he arrives at the Quenus' house. He is reluctant to take the job as inspector at the fish market that Gavard secures for him because finds the smells and the fishwives difficult to stomach, and the abundance of food that he sees everywhere in Les Halles bothers him. He gives some of his salary to Verlaque because of his sense of honour, his altruism and his naivety. He is also the one who teaches Muche to read. He is tender and shy with women, constantly haunted by the memory of the young woman who died in his arms and who seems to be the only one he ever loved.

After his plans were thwarted by his mother's death and he was wrongly condemned by a flawed justice system, Florent may seem very fragile, but he is actually brave and determined. He nurtures the same republican idealism as he did prior to his stint in the penal colony and continues his fight. He becomes the leader of the conspirators at Lebigre's bar and plans the uprising down to the finest details, before being betrayed and arrested. Like Eugène Lantier, the "Thin" character from *Germinal* who leaves the mine after the failure of the strike, Florent leaves

Les Halles after the uprising fails.

The other republicans, namely Charvet, Clémence, the hunchback Logre and Lacaille are also "Thin" characters who fight against the bourgeois system.

## Mademoiselle Saget

Mademoiselle Saget is a different kind of "Thin" character. Instead of opposing the "Fat" characters, she relies on them for her survival and trades secrets and gossip for the food she slips into her basket. She is a small, withered, devious and malicious old woman who spies on everyone in the neighbourhood from her home in the Rue Pirouette and spreads vicious slander about them.

# ANALYSIS

## NATURALISM

The new literary and artistic movement of realism emerged in Europe in the mid-19th century. It was characterised by the desire to imitate reality: the writers of this movement aimed to be as objective as possible. They no longer sought to idealise the things they described, but rather to depict reality as it was. Some writers pushed realism even further, giving rise to another movement, naturalism, of which Zola was the leading figure.

Zola aimed to go beyond realism, which is based on observing and reproducing reality, by applying the experimental scientific methods of his time, and in particular those of the doctor Claude Bernard (1813-1878), to his writing. This approach is particularly evident in the vast cycle of the *Les Rougon-Macquart* novels, which bears the subtitle "Natural and social history of a family under the Second Empire". Bernard's approach involved passing through the stages of observation, hypothesis and experiment. Similarly, Zola observed reality, put forward a hypothesis and tested it through experimentation: in his books, he depicts the events which stem from particular individuals being placed in a specific environment. In the *Les Rougon-Macquart* cycle, the hypothesis he is trying to prove is that individuals' fates are shaped by the dual determining factors of biological heredity and environmental influence.

The naturalist aesthetic can be seen in *The Belly of Paris* through the meticulous description of its setting, the new central markets of Les Halles, which are a character in their own right and influence the behaviour of the people who sell their wares there.

Although Les Halles looks bright, clean and modern from the outside, a glance below the surface reveals its sordid underbelly: the barbaric violence inflicted on the animals whose throats are cut, illicit love affairs and the basest instincts. Les Halles is like a vast stomach which devours the most delicious dishes and most sumptuous fruits, but which then churns that food out in a sickening tumult of digested waste, crushed sheep's heads, decapitated chickens, spilled blood and rotten vegetables. All the market sellers nourish this monster and end up resembling it: they demonstrate the same violence, insatiable appetite, hypocrisy and contrast between honourable, pleasant appearances and a barbaric, ruthless soul. Similarly, dark streets, like the Rue Pirouette, whose houses look "like the bellies of pregnant women" (p. 17), in Claude's words, are places where life is lived in the shadows and whose inhabitants are as sordid as their environment. For example, Mademoiselle Saget spies on her neighbours from the window of her apartment, Lebigre's bar, which resembles a brothel, conceals conspirators in its back room, and Gavard hides a vast sum of money in the house of his landlady Madame Léonce.

## THE ART OF DESCRIPTION

Zola is one of the great masters of description in fiction, and he shows off the full extent of his skill in *The Belly of Paris*. Indeed, in this novel the descriptive passages play a greater role in the structure than the narrative passages. There are many descriptions, and they are always put together in the same way:

- Zola begins by providing the reader with an objective description. For example, we are told about the secrets of sausage-making in Quenu's charcuterie, Madame Lecœur's method of making cheap butter and the practice of selling on leftovers from fancy dinners.
- Then, the objective description quickly becomes subjective. A series of metaphors and personifications turn each stall into something of an impressionist painting. For example, in Chapter 1, the description of the vegetables surrounding Florent when he wakes up gives a spring-like impression of freshness and renewal. Conversely, in Chapter 3, the description of the fish is linked to theme of the goldsmith's and jeweller's crafts and creates an atmosphere of gossip and scandal.

This shift from the objective to the subjective gives every description in the novel an obvious symbolic dimension. The market sellers blend into their setting and become one with their products. This can be seen in the description of the Lecœurs' dairy, which suggests a parallel between the foul-smelling cheeses and the equally disgusting comments made by the gossips, Mademoiselle Saget, Madame Lecœur and La Sarriette, when they decide to turn Florent in.

The importance of descriptions in *The Belly of Paris* and their different functions explain the first appearance of Claude Lantier, the misunderstood painter of modernity: Zola uses a painter's style to experience and describe the neighbourhood of Les Halles.

## THE HISTORY OF THE SECOND EMPIRE

All of Zola's novels unfold against the historical backdrop of the Second Empire (1852-1870), and the author constantly criticises the dangerous political situation and corruption of this period.

Specifically, *The Belly of Paris* depicts the popular uprising of February 1848. This second French Revolution put an end to the July Monarchy (1830-1848) and established the Second Republic; similarly, Napoleon III's coup d'état in December 1851 resulted in the creation of the Second Empire. *The Belly of Paris* provides an account of the republican movements, which Florent becomes involved with, and the insurrectional atmosphere that Napoleon III tries in vain to calm.

Finally, the novel offers a precise account of the history of Les Halles. The French architect Victor Baltard (1805-1874) oversaw the construction of this vast commercial building in the heart of Paris between 1852 and 1872. The iron and glass structure of the pavilions of Les Halles symbolises modernity and the industrial era. It is no surprise that they inspire the painter Claude Lantier, who sees them as the embodiment of progress.

# **FURTHER REFLECTION**

## SOME QUESTIONS TO THINK ABOUT...

- Draw up the actantial model of the novel, making sure to include all the characters.
- Study the flashback to Florent's stint in the penal colony and his escape. What are the different functions of this passage?
- What vision of women does Zola present in this novel?
- In what ways can Marjolin and Cadine considered to be allegorical characters?
- In your opinion, who is the main character of the novel, Lisa or Florent? Justify your answer.
- In Chapter 5, study the interplay of dialogue, narrative and description in the passage from "All around them the cheeses were stinking" to "and the géromé kept up the symphony with a sustained high note" (pp. 210-213).
- How is the theme of renewal presented in the episode where Lantier and Florent spend Sunday in Nanterre with Madame François

(Chapter 4)?
- Discuss the naturalism of this novel.

*We want to hear from you!*
*Leave a comment on your online library*
*and share your favourite books on social media!*

# FURTHER READING

## REFERENCE EDITION

- Zola, É. (2009) *The Belly of Paris*. Trans. Nelson, B. Oxford: Oxford University Press.

## REFERENCE STUDIES

- Nelson, B. (2007) *The Cambridge Companion to Zola*. Cambridge: Cambridge University Press.

- Schom, A. (1987) *Emile Zola: A Biography*. London: Queen Anne Press.

## MORE FROM BRIGHTSUMMARIES. COM

- Reading guide – *Germinal* by Émile Zola.

- Reading guide – *L'Assommoir* by Émile Zola.

- Reading guide – *Nana* by Émile Zola.

- Reading guide – *The Earth* by Émile Zola.

- Reading guide – *The Fortune of the Rougons* by Émile Zola.

- Reading guide – *The Ladies' Paradise* by Émile Zola.

- Reading guide – *Thérèse Raquin* by Émile Zola.

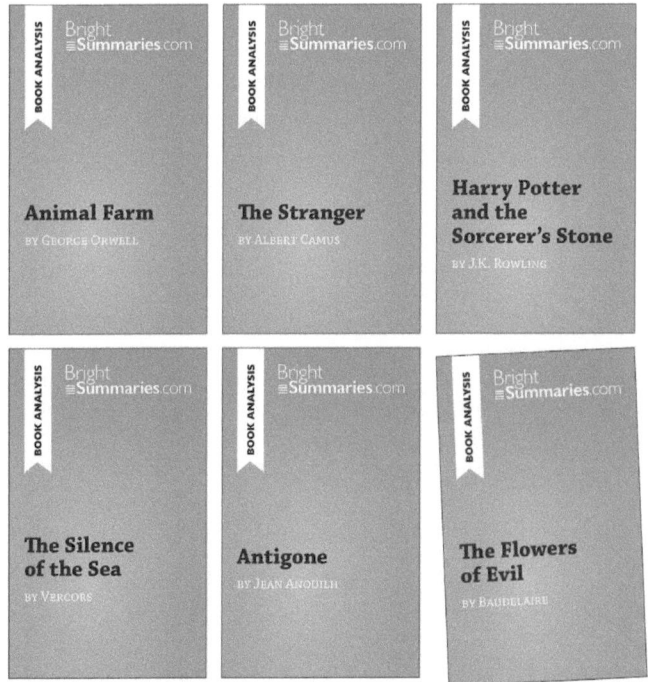

Although the editor makes every effort to
verify the accuracy of the information published,
BrightSummaries.com accepts no responsibility for
the content of this book.

www.brightsummaries.com

Ebook EAN: 9782806296320

Paperback EAN: 9782806296337

Legal Deposit: D/2017/12603/208

Cover: © Primento

Digital conception by Primento, the digital partner of
publishers.